30 Fun Ways to Learn About Music

by Anice Paterson and David Wheway

With contributions from
Glenda Manchanda, Huber Heights, Ohio;
Stephanie Person, Kingsburg, California; and
NeVada Lynn Runnebaum, Leavenworth, Kansas.

30 FUN WAYS
to Learn About
MUSIC

ANICE PATERSON & DAVID WHEWAY
ILLUSTRATED BY K. WHELAN DERY

© 2011 Gryphon House, Inc.
Published by Gryphon House, Inc.
10770 Columbia Pike, Suite 201
Silver Spring, MD 20901
800.638.0928; 301.595.9500; 301.595.0051 (fax)

Visit us on the web at www.gryphonhouse.com
Originally published in 2009 by by A&C Black Publishers Limited; first published in the UK in 2005 by Featherstone Education

Illustrations: K. Whelan Dery
Cover Art: © iStockphoto LP 2009. All rights reserved. iStockphoto® and iStock® are trademarks of iStockphoto LP. Flash® is a registered trademark of Adobe Inc. www.istockphoto.com.

Many thanks to Belleville Primary School

Library of Congress Cataloging-in-Publication Data
Paterson, Anice.
  30 fun ways to learn about music / by Anice Paterson and David Wheway ; with contributions from Glenda Manchanda, Stephanie Person, and NeVada Lynn Runnebaum.
      p. cm.

 Includes bibliographical references and index.
 ISBN 978-0-87659-368-4
  1. School music—Instruction and study—Activity programs. 2. Games with music. I. Wheway, David. II. Manchanda, Glenda. III. Person, Stephanie. IV. Runnebaum,   NeVada Lynn. V. Title. VI. Title: Thirty fun ways to learn about music.
 MT948.P37 2010
 372.87'044--dc22
                                        2010045548

Bulk purchase
Gryphon House books are available for special premiums and sales promotions as well as for fund-raising use. Special editions or book excerpts also can be created to specification. For details, contact the Director of Marketing at Gryphon House.

Disclaimer
Gryphon House, Inc. and the author cannot be held responsible for damage, mishap, or injury incurred during the use of or because of activities in this book. Appropriate and reasonable caution and adult supervision of children involved in activities and corresponding to the age and capability of each child involved is recommended at all times. Do not leave children unattended at any time. Observe safety and caution at all times.

Contents

Introduction

In addition to showing how music is fun and enjoyable for everyone, the activities in this book also show the direct relationship between music and many other areas of development, including literacy, number sense, physical coordination, collaboration with others, concentration, and self-confidence.

On each page you will find:

- Clearly identified learning objectives,
- Key vocabulary for the activity,
- Materials you will need,
- Instructions to guide you through the activity, and
- Suggestions to expand the activity if you want to do more.

In every activity, movement is used as a way of internalizing a sense of rhythm and beat, and of cultivating feelings in response to music. Of equal importance, because listening skills are essential for all learning, every activity provides opportunity for children to practice careful, attentive listening.

- You do not need instruments to make music. Clapping or tapping a rhythm on your knees or a table is enough to sing or dance to. The important things are participation and enjoyment.
- When you use instruments, establish simple ground rules to help children play the instruments without making too much noise that might disturb the other children in the room or others in the building. Apply the ground rules consistently.

Learning Objectives

Music develops children's creativity by encouraging them to:

- Recognize and explore how sounds change,
- Sing simple songs from memory,
- Recognize repeated sounds and sound patterns,
- Match movements to music,
- Use their imaginations,
- Respond in a variety of ways to what they hear, and
- Express and communicate their ideas, thoughts, and feelings by using a variety of songs and instruments.

Music develops children's social skills, including how to work together, share, and cooperate, by developing the ability to:

- Be confident to try new activities, initiate ideas, and speak in a familiar group;
- Maintain attention, concentration, and sit quietly when appropriate; and
- Work as part of a group or class, taking turns and sharing fairly.

Music develops children's communication, language, and literacy skills by encouraging them to:

- Interact with others and take turns;
- Listen attentively, responding to what they hear;
- Listen with enjoyment to songs and other music, stories, rhymes, and poems;
- Make up their own stories, songs, rhymes, and poems; and
- Use language to imagine and recreate roles and experiences.

Music develops children's math skills by encouraging them to:

- Recognize, create, and recreate simple patterns.

Music develops children's physical skills by encouraging them to:

- Move with imagination,
- Move with control and coordination,
- Become aware of the space around themselves and others, and
- Use a range of small and large instruments.

Music and Learning

Just as making and listening to music uses both sides of the brain, responding to music uses both sides of the body. As a child claps, stamps, walks, jumps, skips, dances, and plays simple instruments, the entire brain is stimulated as the entire body is brought into the action.

Enjoying Music with Young Children

You may imagine that you need perfect pitch and an ability to play tuned instruments to have musical experiences with children. This is not true!

The secret of successful music-making with children is to relax and enjoy yourself. If you are having fun, the children will have fun, too. If you play music and sing songs you like, they will join in and sing along with you.

Encourage children to be inventive with sounds, to use different voices in stories, to sing as they work and play, and to use sound-makers as naturally as they use scissors and paintbrushes. In this way, music will become a natural part of your day, not a special activity taught by certain adults at particular times in particular places.

Ten Tips for Successful Musical Experiences

❶ Relax and enjoy the music.

❷ Play music at different times of the day, not just in music sessions.

❸ Play all kinds of music.

❹ Use different voices when you tell stories.

❺ Encourage children to talk, sing, and make sounds as they work and play.

❻ Play listening games and make sure children know when it is "listening time."

❼ Movement adds power to music and reinforces learning. Using both hands or both feet is particularly effective.

❽ Sound-makers don't have to be expensive. Homemade and found items are just as good.

❾ Practice all kinds of rhythm: clapping, tapping, slapping, stamping, marching, clicking, and patting.

❿ Your example as a relaxed music-maker is the best teacher.

Music Activities

C-U-C-K-O-O

cymbal

swoooosh!

drum

sound wave drum

piano

tambourine

maracas

triangle

castanet

Shake It Around

Listening and really hearing different sound qualities cultivates attention and responsiveness. Moving in a group develops sensitivity to other people.

Vocabulary

copy

drum

instrument

listen

play

practice

shake

smooth

sound

tambourine

tap

tiptoe

wiggle

xylophone

What you need

- space for the children to move around
- 3–4 distinctive instrumental sounds—for example, shaking a tambourine, tapping a drum, and playing a xylophone

Learning objectives

Children will:

- Move with control and coordination.
- Match their movements to music.
- Develop a feeling for the qualities of sounds.
- Respond to sounds with body movements.

What you do

❶ Play each sound to the children and ask them to show how it makes them want to move.

❷ As a group, choose three or four good moves and practice the actions together. For example:

- Shaking the tambourine—shake hands in the air,
- Tapping the drum—walk on tiptoe, and
- Playing a scale on the xylophone—move smoothly around the room.

❸ Play the sounds in different sequences, and have the children move and respond accurately to the sounds.

Another idea

- Children could paint or draw in time to the music. Tapping a drum might produce a "dotty" picture. Shaking a tambourine might produce a zigzag picture.

The Key to It All

Listening to an interesting sound and responding with just your fingers is a lesson in concentration, listening, and fine motor control.

Vocabulary

fingers
long
loud
pattern
reflect
regular
shake
short
soft
wiggle

What you need

● set of keys that makes a good noise

Learning objectives

Children will:

● Move with control and coordination.
● Match movements to music.
● Respond to a sound, reflecting on the quality of the sound.

What you do

❶ Have the children sit on the carpet. Tell them to hold their arms out in front and wiggle their fingers.

❷ Shake the keys, and ask everyone to wiggle their fingers to the beat.

❸ Shake the keys in a variety of ways; for example, vigorously, gently, for a long time, for a short time, in a regular pattern, and so on. Encourage the children to move their fingers in a way that reflects the way the sound is made.

More ideas

- Try shaking the keys behind your back or a piece of furniture so the children have to respond to the sound, not the visual stimulus.
- Invite one or two children take a turn shaking the keys.

What a Character!

Use any music you like. It is important that you communicate how much you enjoy the music, so familiarize yourself with any music that you decide to use.

Vocabulary

band
bouncy
ceremony
float
flute
glide
listen
loud
march
mood
parade
skate
strong

What you need

- recorded music with a strong character—for example, brass band marching, floating electronic music, or flute (maximum 2 minutes per extract)

Learning objectives

Children will:
- Listen attentively.
- Respond to music and move with confidence.
- Reflect on the quality of a sound, and move in response to it.

What you do

1. Find a place for children to sit in a circle to start, but with enough space to move around.
2. Play one piece of music for the children to listen to. Have the children move while they sit, to get the feel of the music. Don't encourage big movements at this point.
3. When the music ends, talk about words that could describe it—"strong," "bouncy," "floaty," and so on.
4. Talk about the context of the music—music for outdoors, for parades, for soldiers, for skating, and so on.
5. Choose a suitable event for the music, play it again, and let the children march, skate, or glide around the room!
6. Do the same thing with another selection of music.

More ideas

- March, float, or skate in twos, fours, or even eights. Talk about directions, mood, and the shapes the children made. What is the mood of the people in the music? Are they happy, sad, or serious?
- Try humming or singing part of the music, now that the children are familiar with it.

Keep It Still

4

Vocabulary

bend
down
feel
imagine
listen
lower
pause
raise
slow
still
time

What you need

- small snippet of recorded music with a slow, reflective, drawn-out style—for example, Barber's "Adagio" or Albinoni's "Adagio for Strings"
- space for each child to lie down

Learning objectives

Children will:

- Use their imaginations.
- Respond to music and enjoy what they hear.
- Reflect stillness through the body.

What you do

1. Model for the children how to raise one arm in a very slow movement until it is above the head, and then lower it slowly down again.
2. Do the same while you play the snippet of music, raising and lowering one arm as the music plays.
3. Now have all the children lie down on the floor.
4. Tell the children they can lie still and listen, or move an arm very slowly as you play the music again.
5. Leave a pause at the end of the music, so the children can be still and remember it in their heads. Fade the music to silence; don't turn it off abruptly.
6. Engage the children in a discussion about how the music made them feel.

More ideas

- Do the same activity using both arms, either together or alternating them.
- Try this variation. Start from a standing position, then bend way over with arms hanging down, and, as the music plays, have everyone *slowly* straighten their backs and raise their arms until they are standing with arms above their heads.

Hands

Experiment with sound, rhythm, and pattern in the simplest possible way, using our own bodies as instruments.

Vocabulary

bang
clap
gentle
louder
quiet
repeat
rough
rub
slap
softer
sound
stroke
tap
tiny

What you need

- quiet place and time

Learning objectives

Children will:

- Observe the relationship between movement and sound.
- Explore the sounds and patterns they can make with their hands.
- Extend their vocabularies and explore the meaning of words.

What you do

❶ Have the children sit down on the carpet. Make some tiny sounds with your hands and ask the children to copy them—for example, stroke your hand on your sleeve or tap with your first finger only.

❷ Try the same sounds with the other hand.

❸ Encourage the children to find new sounds with their hands.

❹ Choose some children to demonstrate their sounds.

❺ Find words to describe the sounds, such as "rough," "quiet," and "gentle."

❻ Repeat your favorite sounds to make patterns—for example, rub, rub, pat, pat, rub, rub, pat, pat. . . .

Another idea

● Try the same activity with louder sounds, such as clapping, slapping, and banging. Make more complex patterns, varying loudness and softness as well as sound type.

6 Feet

Experiment with pattern and rhythm on a large scale, and add resonance and excitement to the experience.

Vocabulary

angry
bang
fast
heavy
jump
listen
loud
march
noisy
patterns
silent
slide
slither
slowly
soft/softer
stamp

What you need

- hallway or other uncarpeted big space with a good, resonant, echo-like sound

Learning objectives

Children will:

- Move with confidence.
- Explore sounds and meanings of new descriptive words.
- Understand the relationship between movement and sound.

What you do

❶ Have the children stand up. Invent some slow, heavy sounds that they can make with their feet.

❷ Encourage the children to move around the space slowly and heavily, and guide them to listen to the big sounds they are making.

❸ Now find a slithery, sliding sound and do the same.

❹ Next, have the children find tiny sounds of their own and share them with the group.

❺ See if anyone can make silent movements.

❻ Repeat the best sounds lots of times to make a pattern, such as "loud, loud, soft, soft" or "slither, stamp, stamp, slither."

soft

loud

tap

Another idea

- Find words to describe the sounds and patterns, such as "heavy," "noisy," "fast," "marching," and "angry."

Mouths

Mouth percussion is what we use when we talk. Consonants are the "percussion section" of our language "orchestra."

Vocabulary

click
consonant
explode
fast
faster
hiss
listen
pattern
pop
repeat
slow
slower

What you need

- quiet place and time

Learning objectives

Children will:

- Extend their vocabularies and explore the meaning of new descriptive words.
- Understand that musical patterns come from repeating any sound.

What you do

1. Have the children sit on the carpet. Make the sounds of consonants, such as /p/, /g/, and /t/, as explosively as possible.
2. Repeat the sounds many times to make patterns—for example, "p-p-pooo, p-p-pooo, p-p-pooo," "ch-ch-ch, ch-ch-ch," or "d-d-d-d, b-b-b-b, d-d-d-d, b-b-b-b."
3. Help the children find other ways to make percussion sounds with their mouths, for example, finger popping or clicking their tongues.
4. Try some sounds fast, slow, or repeated in patterns.

More ideas

- Play copycat with the noises, with individual children leading the others.
- Find words starting with the consonants the children know. A little nonsense poem or rhyme might emerge. If it does, concentrate on the repeated patterns rather than meaning, for example, "p-p-poodle-poodle, n-n-noodle-noodle," "ch-ch-ch-ch-ch-ch-chair, ch-ch-ch-ch-ch-ch-chair," and so on.

Sing the Notes

This is a simple musical routine to incorporate into your morning greeting or morning group time. Be sure to use a narrow vocal range with no big leaps. Sing at a high enough pitch for the children's young voices.

Vocabulary

conversation

copy

good morning

greetings

hello

higher/lower

note/notes

pattern

repeat

rhythm

syllable

What you need

- no materials necessary

Learning objectives

Children will:

- Develop confidence in their singing.
- Listen attentively.

What you do

❶ Start by singing two notes for the children to repeat—for example, sing "Hel-lo," a playground chant, or "Cu-ckoo." Sing one note for each syllable, and move back and forth between the two notes you have chosen.

❷ Encourage the children to "answer," using the same pattern and notes.

❸ Move on to a new call when they are used to the first one and can sing it mostly in tune.

Another idea

- Longer "conversations" can be held and more notes can be used once the children get the idea. For example, sing out, "Is your grandma better now?" or "What's your baby brother's name?" Keep the rhythm going, and make it like a real conversation.

Teddy Bear, Teddy Bear

Adding percussion to a simple, familiar rhyme calls for imagination and careful listening.

Vocabulary

around
castanet
drum
gently
ground
light
maracas
night
prayers
rhyme
stairs
tap
teddy bear
triangle
turn
whisk broom

What you need

- percussion instruments or sound-makers
- space to stand and move around

Learning objectives

Children will:

- Match movement to music.
- Play an instrument individually.

What you do

❶ Tell the children that you are going to say a rhyme and they will act it out.

❷ Say the rhyme, encouraging the children to do the appropriate actions with you.

> **Teddy Bear, Teddy Bear**
>
> *Teddy bear, teddy bear,*
> *Turn around.*
> *Teddy bear, teddy bear,*
> *Touch the ground.*
> *Teddy bear, teddy bear,*
> *Go up the stairs.*
> *Teddy bear, teddy bear,*
> *Say your prayers.*
> *Teddy bear, teddy bear,*
> *Turn out the light.*
> *Teddy bear, teddy bear,*
> *Say good night.*

❸ Now choose a percussion sound for each action—for example:

- Turn around—shake maracas.
- Touch the ground—tap rhythm sticks or wooden spoons together.
- Climb the stairs—play low to high on a xylophone.
- Say your prayers—gently tap a triangle.
- Turn out the light—one click of a castanet or a clicker.
- Say good night—a quiet brush of a whisk broom on a drum.

turn around
(maracas)

touch the ground
(sticks)

climb the stairs
(xylophone)

❹ Choose children to play the sounds for each movement.

Another idea

- Try playing the game again, with some of the children making the sounds behind a screen or bookshelf. See if the others can guess the part of the rhyme that corresponds to the sound being played.

10 Move Along, Please

Here, you will play percussion as you sing or chant the verses. This requires the children to listen attentively to each other and to the words.

Vocabulary

baby
bus
chime bar
cymbals
driver
drum
horn
people
pitter-patter
poem
rain/raindrops
shakers
song
swish
thunder
triangle
wheels
wiper

What you need

- songs or poems—for example, "I Hear Thunder," "The Wheels on the Bus," or another song or poem of your choice that has a strong rhythm and words that evoke sounds

Learning objectives

Children will:

- Explore and experiment with sounds and words.
- Work as part of a group.
- Add vocal or percussion sounds to a poem or song.

What you do

❶ Have the children sit on the carpet. Sing the song or say the poem until everyone knows it well from memory.

> I Hear Thunder (Recite this or sing it to the tune of "Frère Jacques.")
> *I hear thunder; I hear thunder,*
> *Oh, don't you? Oh, don't you?*
> *Pitter-patter raindrops,*
> *Pitter-patter raindrops,*
> *I'm wet through.*
> *I'm wet through.*

Wheels on the Bus (Traditional)

The wheels on the bus go 'round and 'round,
'Round and 'round, 'round and 'round.
The wheels on the bus go 'round and 'round,
All around the town.

Additional verses:

The wipers on the bus go swish, swish, swish…
The baby on the bus goes, "Wah, wah, wah"…
People on the bus go up and down…
The horn on the bus goes beep, beep, beep…
The money on the bus goes clink, clink, clink…
The driver on the bus says, "Move on back"…

❷ Talk about appropriate sounds to accompany the poem or song, such as taps on a drum or cymbal, or tingling a triangle.

❸ Make the sounds for each of the groups of people on the bus: shakers for the children, chopsticks for the grandmas' knitting, and triangles for the lights, and so on. For "I Hear Thunder" use drums for the thunder, rainsticks or rattles for the rain, and chime bars for "I'm wet through."

"I hear thunder" (floor drum) "pitter-patter raindrops" (wrist bells) or (maracas)

More ideas

- One or two children play the sounds while everyone else sings.
- Everyone sings and plays instruments together (this is very hard and takes lots of practice!).

Tickle Your Funnybone!

Choral speaking is a traditional way to develop children's sense of rhythm and patterns of speech, and also to develop their listening skills.

Vocabulary

amusing
border
disorder
exaggerate
expression
funny
kangaroo
mood
rhyme
silly
surprised
vexed

What you need

- quiet place and time
- short, light, amusing poem or verse that can be learned quickly—for example, "The Duck and the Kangaroo" or "There Was an Old Man on the Border" by Edward Lear

Learning objectives

Children will:

- Speak clearly and audibly.
- Recite simple poems from memory.
- Develop variety in vocal tone.

What you do

❶ Say one of the following poems until everyone knows it well and can say it rhythmically.

The Duck and the Kangaroo

Said the duck to the kangaroo,
"Good gracious! How you hop!
Over the fields and the water too,
As if you never would stop!"

"Please give me a ride on your back!"
Said the duck to the kangaroo.
"I would sit still and say nothing but 'Quack',
The whole of the long day through!"

There Was an Old Man on the Border

There was an old man on the border,
Who lived in the utmost disorder;
He danced with the cat, and made tea in his hat,
Which vexed all the folks on the border.

❷ Talk about what the song or poem means (if anything). Discuss the mood—funny, amusing, silly—and how the children might exaggerate the words as they speak.

❸ Practice exaggerated expression—for example, the voice going up when you say "'Good gracious! How you hop!" or heavy emphasis when you say "Who lived in the utmost disorder!"

❹ Perform the verse together as a group, exaggerating pitch and expression. Try to make any listener laugh!

More ideas

- Try choral speaking with some other rhymes. Consider familiar nursery rhymes with a strong beat. (For example: "Diddle, diddle dumpling, my son John. . .")
- Divide your group into two sections and have them alternate reciting the lines.

Tones

This simple exercise increases sensitivity to vocal tones, and it is just plain fun to do!

Vocabulary

angry
clenched teeth
count
gentle
happy
harsh
hiss
loud/loudly
quiet
smooth
soft
sweet
tone
voice

What you need

- large space for the children to sit (preferably on carpet), with two children on chairs in the front; later, you will want all the children to sit in pairs, across from each other

Learning objectives

Children will:

- Recognize and explore how sounds can change.
- Count reliably.
- Increase the range of vocal tones they can use to express themselves.

What you do

1. Everyone practices counting together to five, 10, or 20, depending on your group.
2. Discuss how your voice changes when you are angry and when you are happy. Demonstrate by, for example, saying some names in different ways and seeing if they can guess whether you are angry or happy.
3. Choose two children to sit on chairs in the front. Have them sit on their hands so they can focus on their voices.
4. Have the two children count, sounding angry in different ways—for example, very loudly, hissing, or through clenched teeth. How many ways can they sound angry?
5. Repeat with two other children. This time have them count, sounding happy.

More ideas

- Have children sit in pairs across from each other. Each child counts in an angry way and a happy way.
- Discuss the various ways everyone managed to change the tone of his or her voice.

Get Coordinated!

13

There are two parts to this activity. First, developing muscle control, and, second, cultivating an inner body-sense of rhythm. These are closely interrelated.

Vocabulary

beat
coordinated
in time
left
repeat
rhythm
right
together

What you need

- activities for children that use dough or clay, that challenge the children to build constructions, or that use threading and sorting skills

Learning objectives

Children will:

- Develop their fine motor control.
- Develop their sense of rhythm.

What you do

❶ Over time, provide plenty of activities that develop small hand and finger control, such as those that use dough, construction, threading, and sorting. Some days, have the children work on these activities to music with a strong beat, to help them develop an inner sense of rhythm. Encourage the children to tap their feet to the beat.

❷ Try some of the following movement rhymes to help with beat and rhythm:

- "One Potato, Two Potato"—Clench fists on top of each other, and alternate the hands with each count. Do exaggerated movements to emphasize the rhythm.

One Potato, Two Potato

One potato, two potato,
Three potato, four,
Five potato, six potato,
Seven potato, more.

Eight potato, nine potato,
Where is ten?
Now we must count over again.

- "Head, Shoulders, Knees, and Toes"—Sing the song, using the actions to emphasize the rhythm.

Head, Shoulders, Knees, and Toes

Head, shoulders, knees, and toes,
Knees and toes.
Head, shoulders, knees, and toes,
Knees and toes.

Eyes and ears and mouth and nose.
Head, shoulders, knees, and toes,
Knees and toes!

More ideas

- March to music. Concentrate on feeling the left foot/right foot exactly in time.
- Then have everyone "march" in a sitting position, alternating left fist/right fist on their knees to the beat of the music.

14

Let Sleeping Bells Lie

This is about listening carefully, paying attention, and developing fine motor skills as well!

Vocabulary

bells
careful
instrument
jingle
quiet
shake
sleeping
small
sound
still
tambourine

What you need

- instruments, such as bells or a tambourine, that make a sound with the smallest movement

Learning objectives

Children will:
- Sustain attentive listening.
- Move with control.
- Notice that any small movement creates a sound.

What you do

1. Have the children sit in a circle on the carpet. Show them how to make a jingling sound. Let several children (or all of them) jingle the instruments, so they understand the sound.
2. Tell the children that you are going to pass the bells or the tambourine around, but the jingles are sleeping and they need to stay asleep!
3. Pass the instrument around the circle, trying not to jingle at all. Get everyone to listen for a jingle or the slightest sound.
4. When you've tried with one kind of instrument, try again with another.

More ideas

- Try the same activity with the bells or tambourine (or some keys) on the floor in the middle of the circle. Take turns getting the instrument from the center and passing it to someone else, without making a sound!
- Experiment with making the smallest sound you possibly can with the instrument.

How Long Does It Last?

Here is another activity that cultivates concentration, close listening, and auditory discrimination.

Vocabulary

bell
chime bar
cymbal
listen
long
resonant
ring
short
sound
stop

What you need

- cards with words or symbols for the words "long," "short," "ring," and "stop"
- instruments and household or classroom objects made from different materials—for example, a plastic box, wooden spoons, metal spoons, radiator, cymbal, a bell to strike or a chime bar

Learning objectives

Children will:

- Recognize how sounds change.
- Listen acutely and make judgments about the quality of a sound.

What you do

1. Play some of the instruments and sound-makers, and listen for the sounds they make.
2. When the children have listened to some of the sounds, play something with a ringing sound—for example, a chime bar, bell, or cymbal and ask the children to listen for when the sound stops.
3. Next, strike two wooden spoons together and ask the children to listen again.
4. Talk about "long" and "short" sounds, and whether the sound rings (is a resonant sound) or stops quickly (a dead sound).
5. Hold up the "long" and "short" cards. Ask a child to choose a sound-maker and make a single sound. The other children listen and point to the "long" or "short" card. Repeat with the "ring" and "stop" cards.

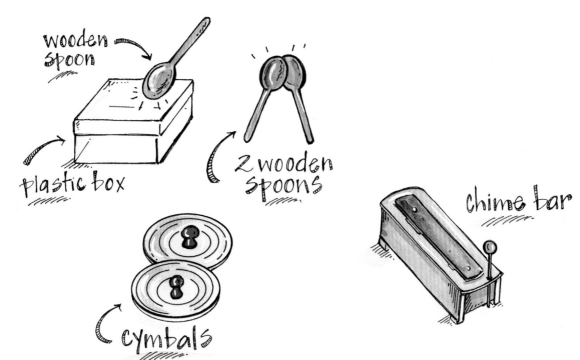

wooden spoon

plastic box

2 wooden spoons

cymbals

chime bar

More ideas

- Organize your sound-makers into those that make short (dead) sounds and those that make long (resonant) sounds.
- Make sound patterns—for example, "short, short, long, long" or "ring, ring, short, (pause), ring, ring, short, (pause)...."

16 I Went to the Store

This will help children think about sounds and find words to describe the sounds.

Vocabulary

castanets
chime bar
cymbal
drum
high
high note
low
piano
shaker
tambourine
triangle

What you need

- range of instruments and sound-makers

maracas   triangle

castanet

Learning objectives

Children will:

- Understand that small movements can make sounds.
- Explore a range of sounds and collect them imaginatively for future use.

What you do

❶ Have the children sit in a circle on the carpet. If the children don't know the game "I Went to the Store and Bought a _____," play it with groceries, toys, or other shopping items first until they know how it works.

❷ When the children understand the format, play the game with musical sounds.

❸ Each child chooses a sound-maker. They say its sound, and then play it. For example:

Child 1: I went to the store and bought a drum "boom" (plays drum).

drum

Child 2: I went to the store and bought a cymbal "clang" (plays cymbal).

cymbal

30 Fun Ways to Learn About Music

Child 3: I went to the store and bought a tambourine "rattle" (plays tambourine).

tambourine

Child 4: I went to the store and bought a chime bar "dong" (plays chime).

chime bar

Child 5: I went to the store and bought a high note (plays on piano or sings high).

piano

Another idea

● Try the same activity cumulatively as each child adds something—for example: I went to the store and bought a cymbal "clang", a lion's "roar", a triangle "cling", and a drum "boom." Each child plays the sound as they say the sequence.

What's Different?

Paying attention to the emotional mood of a piece of music is an important step towards self-awareness and towards appreciation for all kinds of musical expression.

Vocabulary

bouncy
cheerful
dance
different
fast
jolly
loud
mournful
sad
same
slow
soft

What you need

- 2 contrasting pieces of recorded music (one minute each)—for example, loud and cheerful/slow and mournful; brass band/blues song; bouncy pop song/ballad or love song; jolly dance/slow dance

Learning objectives

Children will:

- Communicate ideas, thoughts, and feelings.
- Respond to what they hear.
- Develop musical memory and the ability to distinguish sounds and patterns of sounds.

What you do

1. Have the children sit on the carpet. Play one of the pieces. Talk about it, using open-ended questions such as, "What can you hear?" "What do you think they were feeling as they played the music?" "What does the music sound like to you?"

2. Play the music more than once, incorporating some movement (see "What a Character!" on page 16).

3. Tell the children you are going to play another piece of music, and ask them to listen for what is different about it. Play it once, and then play it again. Talk about it, using more open-ended questions, such as, "What did you hear?" "What was different?" "How did you feel when you were listening?"

4. Use the same two pieces again at quiet times during the next few days, perhaps when the children are coming in, during snack time, or in the listening corner, so they get to know them well.

cheerful

sad

loud

More ideas

- Play a little bit more of the piece each time you use it, but always start at the beginning.
- Be sure to tell the children what the music is called.

Five Green Bottles

18

Patterns are very important in all music-making. In this song, children can take what they know about counting and "put it in reverse." Each verse repeats the same pattern.

Vocabulary

backward
count
forward
left
listen
numbers 1–5 and
   1–10
one less
turn

What you need

- 5 (10 when the children can count backward from 10) green plastic bottles

Learning objectives

Children will:
- Sing a song from memory, noting the pattern.
- Say and use number names in familiar contexts.
- Count backward from five (or 10).

What you do

❶ Learn the first verse of "Five Green Bottles" slowly, making sure that it is pitched high enough for the children to be able to sing the notes.

> **Five Green Bottles**
> Five green bottles
> Hanging on the wall,
> Five green bottles
> Hanging on the wall,
> And if one green bottle
> Should accidentally fall,
> There'll be four green bottles
> Hanging on the wall.

❷ Talk about how the numbers go backward.

❸ Now sing all the verses, using the bottle props to help and pausing each time to count how many bottles are left.

④ Count the remaining bottles each time until the children know the song really well.

⑤ When the children can sing "Five Green Bottles," let them take turns removing a bottle for each verse and counting how many are left.

⑥ When they are ready, progress to "Ten Green Bottles."

Another idea

- This game also works with "Ten in the Bed" (try with soft toys under a blanket), or any other similar poem.

Ten in the Bed
There were ten in the bed,
And the little one said,
"Roll over, roll over!"
So they all rolled over
And one fell out.

There were nine in the bed...

19 Do It Again

This activity is another way to experiment with musical pattern-making. It also introduces the concept of "reading" music in a very simple way.

Vocabulary

bells
chime bar
instrument
large
less
long
loud
more
pattern
repeat
shaker
short
small
soft
symbol
tambourine

What you need

- pictures of each instrument (several for each instrument, large and small sizes) glued to cards
- 3–4 instruments or sound sources—for example, tambourine, shaker, bells, chime bar

Learning objectives

Children will:
- Practice turn-taking.
- Recognize repeated sounds and patterns.
- Learn that in music, as in English, we read from left to right.
- Learn that symbols can be used for sounds.

What you do

❶ Spend some time looking at the instruments and experimenting with the sounds they make.

❷ Practice playing each one loudly, quietly, for a long time, for a short time, and try making a pattern with the sounds.

❸ When the children are familiar with the instruments, show them the pictures, naming each picture and talking about the sizes of the pictures.

❹ Lay out three or four cards, all the same size, and ask the children to play the appropriate instruments as you point to each card.

❺ Lay out the same cards, plus one small one, and see whether the children can play loud and soft as you point to the cards. (Large = loud, small = soft.)

❻ Now let the children experiment by laying out patterns to play themselves or for other children to play.

More ideas

- Leave this activity set up in a quiet area so the children can play independently. Give them some blank cards, too, to indicate pauses in the music.
- As they become more adept, try the challenge of having two groups, and creating a "call and response" pattern. (Example: Group 1—loud, loud, soft; loud, loud, soft, (pause). Group 2—soft, soft (pause) Repeat this group-to-group pattern several times.

Birds, Beasts, and Butterflies

Thinking about animals and their characteristics is an imaginative way to connect feelings with music.

Vocabulary

castanets

deep

drum

fast

guitar

heavy

high

imagination

keyboard

large

light

low

piano

scraper

slow

triangle

What you need

- large cards with pictures of animals, birds, and butterflies
- variety of sound-makers (castanets, triangle, drum, scrapers, bells, including very deep/low sounds—for example, low notes on a piano, keyboard, drum, or guitar)

Learning objectives

Children will:

- Use their imaginations.
- Learn that in music, as in English, we read from left to right.
- Develop an understanding of simple symbols for sounds.

What you do

❶ Make some birds, beasts, and butterflies cards. (Invite the children to draw the pictures.)

❷ Look at the cards and talk about the creatures. Talk about the kind of sound each might make. How big is it? How does it move? Can it fly? Is it scary?

❸ Choose two cards for the session (perhaps an elephant and a butterfly).

❹ Decide on instruments and voice sounds for each—for example, low drums and trumpet sounds played very slowly for an elephant; triangles or bells played very fast for butterflies.

❺ Two groups of children play and make sounds for each picture, repeating them lots of times.

❻ Now try with each group playing when their sign is up, and stopping when it is down.

left to right

kids' drawings

butterfly

bird

elephant

More ideas

- Leave the cards in your music corner for the children to use on their own. Add some blank cards for their own ideas.
- You might want to introduce excerpts from Saint-Saens' "Carnival of the Animals" or Prokofiev's "Peter and the Wolf" along with this activity.

21

What's Your Name, Again?

By playing this simple game with the sounds of their names, the children will be reinforcing the rhythmic link between music and words.

Vocabulary

different
pattern
repeat
rhyme
rhythm
same
sound

What you need

● no materials needed

Learning objectives

Children will:

● Make up their own rhymes.
● Explore and experiment with sounds and words.
● Make simple rhythms and sound patterns.

What you do

❶ Have the children sit on the carpet. Talk to them about the sounds and rhythms of their own names.

❷ Talk about other names, and point out ones that rhyme—for example: Sam/Pam, Ron/Jon, Millie/Jilly, Karen/Sharon.

❸ Repeat a name over and over and put it in a pattern:

> Daisy, Daisy, Daisy, Kishan, Kishan,
> Daisy, Daisy, Doh, Kishan, Kishan, Go!

❹ Use several names to make a rhythm or rhyme:

> Murali, Giri, Jimmy, and Joe,
> Ella and Lana and Freya and Mo.

❺ Sing the rhymes in little tunes, repeating each line until it ceases to sound like the names.

❻ Add a simple beat on a tambourine or rhythm sticks to keep the rhythm going.

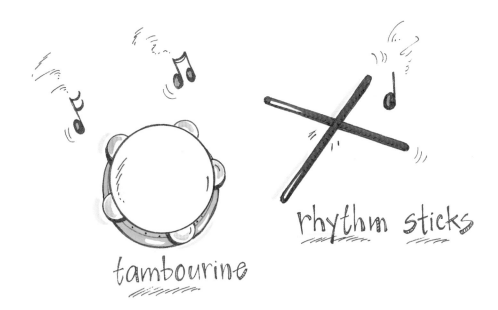

tambourine

rhythm sticks

More ideas

● Groups of children can make up their own rhymes, then "perform" them to each other. It is important to practice several times before performing for someone.

● Try playing this game with the names of characters in favorite books, too.

22 Grandfather, Father, and Son

As you tell this little story in rhythm and rhyme, beat the drum, and move in time to the beat, you are creating for the children a whole-body experience, which is the very foundation of music.

Vocabulary

beat
fast/faster
hurry
in time
rhyme
slow down
slowly
speed up
start
stop

What you need

● drum or drums

Learning objectives

Children will:
● Respond with enjoyment to rhymes and poems.
● Use their imaginations.
● Feel different speeds and moods and convey them through movement.

What you do

❶ Teach the children the following rhyme:

> *Slowly, slowly walks my grandpa,*
> *Leaning hard upon his stick,*
> *"Wait for me, my dear," says grandpa,*
> *"I'm too old, I can't be quick."*

❷ In a big space with room to move, beat the drum slowly while the children walk slowly like Grandpa. As they move in time, repeat the rhyme.

❸ Speed up the drum beat and ask, "Who is walking now?" As the children move faster, say this part of the rhyme:

> *Father goes to work each morning,*
> *This is how he walks along.*

bent forward

leaning on stick

drum

shuffle

❹ Speed up the drum beat and ask, "Who is walking now?" As the children move faster, say this part of the rhyme:

Off to school I, have to hurry,
Going down the road I run.

Another idea

● Make up another poem about Grandma, Mom, and Me, or Aunt, Cousin, and Me. Use other instruments to vary the sound for each character in the poem (triangle, tambourine, and xylophone).

Animal Fair

23

You will find many ways to use this familiar song to introduce and reinforce both simple and complex experiences with rhythm.

Vocabulary

accompaniment

actions

animal

baboon

beasts

beat

elephant

fair

"in time"

monkey

repeat

rhyme

rhythm

What you need

● instruments that can be played softly, such as rhythm sticks, chime bars, and bells

Learning objectives

Children will:

● Express ideas using imaginative movement.

● Match movements to music.

● Explore and experiment with sounds and words.

What you do

❶ Have the children sit on the carpet with plenty of space around them. Teach them the words to the song "Animal Fair."

Note: If you do not know the tune, say it as a rhyme, or go to websites such as songsforteaching.com or kididdles.com to hear the melody.

> Animal Fair
>
> *I went to the animal fair, all the birds and the beasts were there.*
> *The big baboon by the light of the moon was combing his auburn hair.*
> *The monkey fell out of his bunk, and slid down the elephant's trunk.*
> *The elephant sneezed and fell on his knees.*
> *But what became of the monkey, monkey, monkey…?*

❷ Think of some actions for parts of the song—for example, "birds and beasts" or "fell on his knees." Practice the song and movements until the children know them well.

bird

beast

grrr

...fell on his knees

③ Now try repeating "monkey, monkey, monkey," as a rhythm. If there are two adults, try singing in two groups, with one group singing "monkey, monkey" while the others sing the verse.

④ Try playing the "monkey, monkey" rhythm on rhythm sticks or a chime bar as the children sing the song.

⑤ Let children take turns playing the accompaniment, helping them keep in time.

Another idea

● For older children, try the same activity with the children clapping or slapping their knees as they sing.

24 Peace at Last

As the children work together in a group to create and perform this story with sound effects, they are learning to cooperate and listen to each other.

Vocabulary

high
loud
low
perform
soft
sound effect

What you need

- carpet or a circle of chairs
- *Peace at Last* by Jill Murphy (or another story with repetitive elements and opportunities for making sounds)
- variety of sound-makers

Learning objectives

Children will:

- Use their imaginations to respond to a story.
- Explore sounds and words.
- Begin to develop a sense of sequence, structure, and performance.

What you do

❶ Read the story to the children.

❷ Talk about the parts of the story that suggest sound effects, and ask the children to suggest which sounds would fit.

❸ Pick a few key parts of the story, gather your sounds, practice them, and discuss how they work. For example:

- Going to bed—a xylophone or piano played slowly, low to high

- Snoring—a scraper, or vocal snoring sounds

- Clock—pencils or rhythm sticks tapped together

- Walking—fingers tapped on the floor
- Owl—vocal owl hoot
- Birds—bells shaken gently

- Alarm—bells played loudly and whole group "drrringgg!"

❹ Agree on who is making which sound effect, and when.

❺ Read the story again and "perform" with sound effects.

Another idea

- Find an audience for your story with sound effects—another class or group, or family members and caregivers at pick-up time.

25 Goldilocks

A sensitivity to higher and lower sounds, as well as to louder and softer ones, enhances the children's ability to express themselves in speech and to interpret speech they hear.

Vocabulary

high
low
names of
    instruments
perform
pitch
repeat
sound
tone of voice

What you need

- story of "Goldilocks and the Three Bears"
- variety of instruments and sounds suitable for the key elements in the story

Learning objectives

Children will:

- Respond to stories and explore sounds.
- Develop the ability to discriminate between higher and lower sounds.
- Experience a performance.

What you do

❶ Read or tell the story of "Goldilocks and the Three Bears" and then discuss the tone of voice used to indicate the three bears and their different sizes.

❷ Discuss the different pitches and what would be good sounds to use for each bear, bowl, chair, and so on. Some examples of sounds to try:

- The forest—vocal sounds of wind in trees or birds twittering
- The three bowls—three wood blocks (or bowls and spoons) with three different pitches

tweet!
tweet!

bowls & spoons

- The three chairs—three triangles or chimes, with three different pitches getting higher

- The three beds—three shakers or piano notes
- The three bears—speaking in three different voices or pitches
- Goldilocks—a tune on chime bars, made especially for her

❸ Decide who is going to play what, and when. Practice the parts where the sounds come in.
❹ Read the story through again with the sounds played by the children in a "performance."

Another idea

- Find an audience of other children for an informal concert.

26 Story Trails

Let the sounds tell the story.

Vocabulary

birds singing
bouncy
character
ducks
high
low
musical picture
pointer
sequence
slide
sound
splash
trail

What you need

- large whiteboard *or* paper on an easel *or* flip chart
- variety of instruments and sound-makers

Learning objectives

Children will:

- Develop an understanding of story sequence.
- Use a simple musical structure.
- Begin to develop control of sounds and patterns of sounds in sequence.

What you do

❶ Tell the children that you are going to make a musical story trail together. Decide where to visit for an imaginary musical trail, or use a recent visit to the park, the zoo, or the store.

❷ Talk about the parts of the visit the children liked best—the monkeys at the zoo, splashing in the puddles at the park, the electric doors at the store.

❸ Brainstorm some sounds and sound-makers for their favorite parts. Don't forget voice and body sounds! For example:

- The monkeys—vocal noises or a bouncy drum

drum

30 Fun Ways to Learn About Music

- The puddles—a cymbal

cymbal

- The doors—running a beater up a xylophone or voice "swoooshes"

swooosh!

❹ Decide who will make the walking sound as the trail goes on (slapping on thighs, beat on a drum, and so on).

sound wave drum

❺ Try out the sounds. Decide who will play them, and when.

❻ Draw a map of the musical trail on the whiteboard, paper, or chart, with pictures for each sound. Follow the trail with a pointer. The children play their sounds when the pointer reaches their picture.

More ideas

- Choose somewhere else to visit and make up a different musical trail.
- Leave the trail out so children can play on their own.

Sticky Dancing

As the children explore the strange new sensation of "sticky feet," they become more consciously aware of their own muscles and body movements.

Vocabulary

dance
demonstrate
duct tape
fast
slow
sticky

What you need

- dance music (with a fast tempo)
- duct tape

Learning objectives

Children will:

- Explore and experiment with music and movement.
- Develop body awareness.

What you do

1. Tell the children they are going to do a sticky dance.
2. Roll a piece of duct tape (sticky side out) around your shoe to demonstrate.
3. Put the duct tape around the children's shoes, and have them take a few steps to get used to the feeling of the duct tape.
4. Start the music and invite the children to dance. Encourage them to have fun!
5. When the children are finished dancing, turn off the music and remove the duct tape.

Another idea

● Play a "freeze" game with the music. Start the music as before, and have the children dance. When you stop the music, the children have to freeze. Who can stay still the longest?

28 Rhythm Memory

To be able to hear and reproduce a rhythmic pattern is a sophisticated skill that reinforces both listening and memory.

Vocabulary

beat
circle
clap
remember
rhythm
turn

What you need

● no materials needed

Learning objectives

Children will:
● Recognize repeated sounds.
● Develop musical memory and the ability to distinguish sounds and patterns of sounds.

What you do

❶ Sit with the children in a circle on the carpet. Begin a rhythm by clapping three times, or make a similar pattern that the children can follow.

❷ The child sitting next to you copies your pattern, and adds another rhythm with three more beats.

❸ The next child copies what has been created so far, and adds three more beats, in a different rhythm.

❹ Then, with the teacher leading, everyone repeats the entire nine-beat rhythm until the pattern is clear and steady.

❺ Continue this game, starting again with two different children.

❻ Continue around the circle until everyone has had a turn.

❼ See if the children can repeat each of the rhythms. This will be a challenge!

listening

clap

Another idea

- Vary the activity by asking each child to add a body movement, rather than a rhythm to the pattern. Continue around the circle as above, until everyone has had a turn.

29 Pop! Goes the Weasel

Here is a great example of finding musical instruments where we least expect them. The children will love experimenting with these surprising sound-makers.

Vocabulary

button
circle
cobbler
floor
lid
pop
thumb
weasel

What you need

● metal lids from jars with a safety pop-up button (about 2" in diameter), at least 1 per child, or plastic bottles with an up-open, down-closed top

Learning objectives

Children will:
● Explore and experiment with sound.
● Respond to sound.

What you do

❶ In advance, send a note home with the children asking parents to send in clean jar lids that fit inside the child's hand.

❷ Have the children sit in a circle on the floor, and ask each child to choose a lid. Show the children how to hold the lids and "pop" the button with their thumbs. Talk about the sound.

❸ Sing "Pop! Goes the Weasel," and use these interesting percussion "instruments" to "POP!" at the right place in the verses.

> **Pop! Goes the Weasel**
> All around the cobbler's bench
> The monkey chased the weasel.
> The monkey thought 'twas all in fun—
> Pop! Goes the weasel.

Johnny has the whooping cough,
Mary has the measles.
That's the way the money goes—
Pop! Goes the weasel.

A penny for a spool of thread,
A penny for a needle.
That's the way the money goes—
Pop! Goes the weasel.

All around the mulberry bush,
The monkey chased the weasel.
That's the way the money goes—
Pop! Goes the weasel.

More ideas

- Think of other songs to sing, using these lids as accompaniment or as sound effects. Or make up new verses for "Pop! Goes the Weasel."
- Use the lids as percussion instruments in other ways. Strike them with a pencil, hit two together like small cymbals, and so on. Have fun with them!

30 Musical Hoops

This activity cultivates listening skills, and encourages rhythmic movement and cooperation.

Vocabulary

cooperation
hula hoop
share
start
stop

What you need

- 6–9 hula hoops
- large space for children to dance and move
- music (fast tempo)

Learning objectives

Children will:

- Move with control and coordination.
- Match movements to music.
- Respond to sounds with body movements.

What you do

1. Gather the children together on the carpet. Explain that when the music is playing, they can dance and move to the music. When the music stops, they need to stand inside a hula hoop.
2. Start the music.
3. After letting it play for a 30–60 seconds, stop the music.
4. Encourage the children to help each other find a hula hoop.
5. When everyone is standing inside a hula hoop, remove one of the hoops.
6. Repeat Steps 2 and 3 until there are only three hula hoops left. This game encourages cooperation. No one should be left out.

   Note: When doing this activity with a large number of children, increase the beginning number of hula hoops and the number left at the end so it is safe to continue to play the game.

hula hoop

More ideas

- Instead of fast music, use slow music to give the children a different experience.
- Make paper tube shakers or paper plate shakers. Record the children playing their shakers, and then use this music to play the game.

Additional Suggestions

Using recorded music

When selecting music to play in your classroom, use music you like, but be sure that children hear a range of different moods and styles. Start by limiting the music to no more than a minute each, gradually increasing the length to build up the children's stamina for listening. Play the same music often, so the children get to know it well. Give it a name, so the children can ask, "When are we going to hear '_____' again?"

Using your body as an instrument

You can make music using anything at all as a sound source! It just has to be organized in a pattern, or repeated in different ways, and you have music.

Using song

Experiencing music should be a regular, relaxed activity during which you and the children do not feel self-conscious. Singing is as natural as breathing and speaking. It should always take place in a positive, non-competitive atmosphere that reinforces a sense of community.

It takes a long time for vocal chords to develop so children can reliably sing in tune. However, just because they can not yet sing in tune does not mean they are not "musical"!

With young children, singing is best when:

- It is unaccompanied—music from a piano makes it harder for children to hear their own voices.
- It is in a narrow vocal range with no big leaps.
- Songs are sung at a high enough pitch for their young voices.
- Songs are learned by heart.
- Songs are sometimes combined with movement and percussion.
- Children stand up to sing, so they can breathe easily.
- Children stand close together for confidence.

Sing anything you and the children like and enjoy. Don't forget the traditional songs! New songs are fun, but the old ones are tried-and-true. Try the following songs, as well as your own choices:

Familiar traditional songs such as:

> She'll be Coming 'Round the Mountain
> Daisy, Daisy
> Polly Put the Kettle on
> Ring Around the Rosy

Number and cumulative songs such as:

> One Potato, Two Potato
> Old MacDonald Had a Farm
> There's a Hole in My Bucket

Action and nonsense songs such as:

> If You're Happy and You Know it
> I Went to the Animal Fair

Some children sing at home. Ask if anyone has a song from home to share with the group. Ask parents, family members, and caregivers the same question.

Using other sound sources and instruments

The voice is the most immediate instrument to use with anyone, especially with young children, but a greater variety of musical experience comes with the addition of percussion. Start with some common objects you will find close at hand, such as keys, saucepans, or sticks to develop rhythm and coordination.

Key things to remember when using instruments:

- Good-quality instruments made with good-quality materials produce the most pleasing sounds. If you are buying instruments, buy the best you can afford.
- Have instruments close at hand to reduce the time lost in getting instruments out and putting them away.
- Noise is an inevitable part of music-making! From the start, manage the noise that will inevitably occur by using clear, well-understood signals for stopping and starting, and expecting an immediate response.
- Develop children's coordination skills so they can handle musical instruments confidently and well.
- Help children respect the instruments and treat them with great care.
- Remember, your example is a powerful influence.

Making your own instruments

- Rhythm sticks—Played in pairs. Cut dowel or broom handles into 8" lengths, and let the children help sand them and paint them. Or use wooden spoons, un-sharpened pencils, chopsticks, or fingers to tap out a rhythm.
- Shakers or maracas—Fill a chip canister or empty plastic bottle with a dozen or so dried peas, beans, and pasta shapes. Try sugar and flour for a softer sound. Replace the lid and secure it with tape. Decorate if desired.
- Drums—Use a saucepan, a waste paper basket, a cookie tin, or a large bowl. Putting a lid on a plastic box drum improves the sound greatly.
- Other ideas—Try using a bunch of keys as shakers, a garlic crusher or empty stapler for castanets, and anything pulled along a radiator as a scraper.
- Almost anything will make a sound! Keep repeating the sound and you have a musical pattern.

Using patterns

When making music, you will repeat ideas and rhythms, create patterns, and sing counting songs both forward and backward. In this way, children begin to feel the repeated units. Making musical patterns is very important in all music-making.

Using rhymes and stories

Pattern-making is a way of thinking about music as an abstract activity. Working with stories and words gives another context for music, and provides a framework for musical imagination. Musical story trails (see page 62) offer an approach to telling stories with music, and telling stories with music is the beginning of composing!

Index